Kuji-Kiri and Majutsu

Sacred Art of the Oriental Mage

ISBN: 978-1-926659-29-9

Published by: F.Lepine Publishing

www.Flepine.com

Table of Contents

Introduction

Kuji-Kiri means "Nine symbolic cuts". It is a technique that belongs to the esoteric Buddhist tradition. From the outside, it seems to consist of drawing nine lines in the form of a grid, then drawing a symbol on the grid. In fact, it is the setting in place of nine energy structures, that once activated, can empower a concept represented by the drawn symbol over the grid. This symbol then interacts with what seems to be reality, and modifies the structure of the universe according to the desired effects.

In other words, the nine lines that we draw in Kuji-Kiri, are nine energy concepts that we lay down on a surface or in the air. This grid is empowered when the person who draws the grid has activated the nine powers in his consciousness. At this point, the drawn grid becomes a representation of the matrix of the world, into which you can summon another conceptual energy.

A Kuji-Kiri user is sometimes called a majutsushi, which translates as magician or conjurer. 真 ma = pure; 術 jutsu = art; 仕 shi = user. Thus, user of the pure art. Usually, the Kuji-Kiri users are experienced monks or priests in the Mikkyo (esoteric) Buddhist tradition, such as Shingon, Ten-Daï, or Shugendo. But there is sufficient correspondence with the Taoist ways to suggest that it came to Japan along with Chinese Buddhists who carried the influence of the Taoist ways. Nowadays, it is mostly popular because of Ninjitsu, but ninjas are not the only ones using Kuji-Kiri and Kuji-In.

Kuji-Kiri is not a nine step guide to power. It is not a simple sorcery formula book that will work instantly if you follow a few basic guidelines. Kuji-Kiri is a simple, yet complete art that required devotion and dedication to learn and empower. Once empowered in its user, the Kuji-Kiri system will make a true mage out of a once ordinary person, who can now influence destinies.

A well trained majutsushi can perform exorcisms, help in healing people, develop supernatural abilities, and influence the flow of events of life. Such a user of the pure art is responsible for his usage of the arts of Kuji-Kiri and Majutsu. It is in a state of respect, compassion and devotion that the power of the mage grows.

Notes on Japanese pronunciation: The traditional Japanese symbols used in all majutsu writings and spell-casting, including Kuji-Kiri, are called Kanji. Two other Japanese ways of writing are called Katakana and Hiragana, which are the modern Japanese writing characters, which behave more like an alphabet. Another way of writing Japanese is Romanji, that consists in writing the sounds using the English alphabet to write the pronunciation, so that you can easily reproduce the pronunciation of the words. In this book, next to each kanji symbol, you will find the Romanji spelling, as well as either the Katakana or Hiragana pronunciation, so you can familiarize yourself with the Japanese alphabets. To execute Majutsu and Kuji-Kiri, you must learn the graphical symbols of each kanji you wish to use in a spell, but also the pronunciation of the words, using the Romanji, Katakana and Hiragana pronunciation keys.

Commonly used word: Jutsu

Kanji: 術

Romanji: Jiyutsu (Ji-yu-tsu)

Katakana: ジュツ

Hiragana: じゆつ

We will mostly be using the Katakana key, unless a word is very uncommon in this style, then we will use the Hiragana.

Technical overview

The use of Kuji-Kiri consists of establishing a link with the matrix of the universe, creating a bond between the physical and spiritual realms. We will then use this bond to interact with the various levels of consciousness of the universe.

The majutsushi will seem to draw a grid, but he is in fact plugging together links between all the planes of existence, tapping into the information of physical matter, life force, feelings, emotional experiences, mental thoughts, consciousness, dimensions, and creative processes, all at once. Once the link is established between all the fibers that constitute the universe, the majutsushi will draw a symbol that will be used as a focus to push new information into the structure of the universe, in order to alter it. Drawing the grid is used to make contact with the matrix, and drawing a symbol is used to alter the information, or put new information in it.

To better understand the process, we will provide an example. First, the majutsushi draws a grid of nine lines, following a specific order, while simultaneously invoking the nine powers that they represent. This sets in place the energy structures that will interact with the matrix of the world. First line, RIN, is drawn from left to right, second line, KYO, is drawn from top to bottom. Then, the third line is drawn from left to right, and the fourth from top to bottom, until the nine lines are drawn. This requires a bit of practice with a pen and paper, to get the proportions right when simply weaving with the fingers in midair. The grid has to be drawn while in

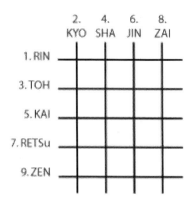

a sacred state of mind, with concentration and willpower. The lines must vibrate with light, and appear in the astral plane. This happens the moment you concentrate and "will" it.

Once the grid is drawn, the user will draw a symbol over the grid. This symbol must also have been previoKujiusly empowered. Let's say in this case, that the symbol of health is used. While the user is drawing, setting in place new energy structures,

he also recites the mantras or formulations associated with each concept, while his mind is absorbed in pure consciousness. If this Kuji-Kiri grid and symbol is drawn on a wound, it will heal faster. Once the grid and symbol are drawn, one must diffuse the conscious modulation of reality in the entire area/organ to affect. The amplitude of the effect depends on the experience and empowerment of the majutsushi.

Once the majutsushi has empowered the nine symbols to create the grid, he can afterwards empower different symbols and conceptual energy patterns to produce various effects. Each time a Kuji-Kiri user empowers a new symbol, he gains a new power. Empowering a new symbol is empowering a complete energy concept, and it requires a bit of time.

The grid and symbol can be drawn with the index and major fingers of the hand, or with a pencil and ink. We most often draw the grid and symbol with the right hand, but it can sometimes be useful to draw with the left hand, on some rare occasions. Before you can draw Kuji-Kiri with your hand, you must empower the sword mudra with your right hand.

So far, we have learned that to perform efficient Kuji-Kiri, we must first:

- Empower the nine Kuji-In energy concepts that make up the grid, allowing us to tap into all planes of existence and use all the tools available to us
- Empower the hand into a magical drawing tool, allowing us to interact with the structure of the universe, so you can use your hand to connect to the fabric of reality and modulate it (load new software in the matrix and run it)
- Empower specific energy concepts represented by symbols

The majutsushi must also have some experience in meditation, and handling un-worded concepts originating in pure thought. This part is unexplainable. It comes naturally with practice and experience. The more you do it, the more you understand its workings.

Empowering Kuji-In

To start empowering the nine Kuji-In energies, you can read other books written on the subject, such as Qi-Gong and Kuji-In, volume 1. The Kuji-In volume 2 and 3 are not required to start with, but will become essential for the serious majutsu-deshi, the student of the pure art. The Kuji-In basics are provided at the end of this book so you can start the empowerment right away.

Empowering the hands

Empower your right hand by making the sword mudra (holding ring and small finger with the thumb, extending the index and major). For 2 minutes, visualize your hand glowing with light, condensing powerful energy with intensity, while repeating the

Japanese words: Riyoku Te Sei, while visualizing the Kanji symbols in your hand. Then, weave your right hand in front of you, drawing the kanji symbols of Power, Hand and Energy (provided on the next page), and imagine that you are actually drawing these symbols into the matrix of the universe. Support the existence of these symbols in the spiritual plane in front of you, when you draw them, by visualizing that the symbols glow with light when you draw them, one over the other. Do not draw the Kuji-Kiri grid yet. Simply draw these symbols in front of you. Right before you are done drawing one symbol, say the corresponding Japanese word aloud. Once the 3 symbols are drawn, stand still again, with your right hand on your lap or in front of you, and focus again on the building up of energies in your hand. Do this 2 minute empowerment of focus and drawing, for at least 3 repetitions, but you can do even more if you wish, to enhance the empowerment. Repeat this empowerment every day for 9 straight days. You may empower the left hand each day, after you have empowered the right.

Learn the first symbol of Power because it is the easiest. Then, when you are ready to learn the second, learn the symbol of Hand. Then, learn the symbol of Energy. This symbol of Energy represents the spirit force Energy, and not the physical strength type of energy; there is something "tangible" to the sense of this Energy symbol, but it remains spiritual Energy.

Power	Hand	Spirit Energy
Riyoku (リョク)	Te (て)	Se-i (セイ)

力　手　精

Empowering tools

Once your hand is empowered, you can use it to empower other tools, such as rice paper, ink, a pen, a brush, or any other object you will be using during your Kuji-Kiri and Majutsu practice. To empower an object, simply establish physical contact with it, or with its container, and visualize the radiant light of power and spiritual energy investing the tools (力精 Riyoku Se-i). You can visualize the symbols in your empowered hand, radiating white light into the empowered tool while the kanji symbols spiritually appear on the tools. If you wish, you can also physically draw these kanji on the tools themselves, but they would only become useful for spiritual empowerment processes. Once the tools are empowered, they will work for any ritual or practice you use them for. This empowerment can take a moment, or a few minutes.

Empowering symbols

Step 1: To empower a symbol, you have to draw it, and meditate on the concept it represents. First, identify the concept it represents without the words to describe it. Get into the feeling of the concept to the best of your ability, and not just the thought of it. Once you have identified these parameters, go on with the next step. Also, find a color that fits with the symbol, for visualization purposes. If you have no idea, use white light. If you can't visualize, then use your imagination in any other way, or simply think about it without the accompanying images.

Step 2: Draw the symbol in front of you, in midair, using your newly empowered hand. In the Japanese language, there is an order and direction to draw each line of a kanji, but this knowledge and experience is not required. If you learn more on Japanese kanji drawing, you will simply have more mental resource invested in the Majutsu, which might make a small difference in the long run. Draw the symbol once, then close your eyes and visualize it in front of you, getting more and more powerful with glowing energy and light. The symbol should stand still in front of you for 10-15 seconds. Then, imagine that the symbol is getting closer to you, slowly, until it enters your third eye (forehead), and dissolves in your brain, then in all your nervous system, over a period of about 10-15 seconds. Use the Japanese word as a mantra, slowly repeating it in your mind.

Draw the symbol a second time in front of you. Let it stand still for 10-15 seconds. Then bring it slowly to your solar plexus. Have the symbol enter your solar plexus and immerse your entire abdomen with its energy. Use the word again as a mantra.

Draw the symbol a third time in front of you. Let it stand still, then visualize the symbol getting bigger and bigger, and bring it into your whole body. Envelope and fill your body with the energy of the symbol. Keep the Japanese words (like a mantra) in your mind.

Step 3: Meditate for at least 15 minutes on the energy and concept of the symbol. Immerse yourself in the feeling of the un-worded thought of this concept. You may look at the symbol as much as it is needed.

When you empowered your hand before, you learned about 3 symbols: Power, Hand and Energy. You can start with these three symbols if you wish to practice with the basics. Here are a few other basic symbols for you to learn and empower.

Health	Happiness	Peace
Ken (ケン)	Fuku (フク)	Ta-i (タイ)

健 福 泰

A few other symbols are contained in this guide. Some will be accompanied with their suggested color, definition, and philosophical contemplation for a maximum empowerment. When no color is suggested, use your feeling and experience. In fact, even when suggested colors are trustworthy choices, you still have to base your choice on your experience and knowledge of Kuji-In. You can't become a user of the pure art by limiting yourself to a guide, but you should consider the wisdom contained in this guide until you are experienced enough to make your own choices.

To empower a symbol, more than one session of 15 minutes will be required. Right from its first empowerment meditation, a symbol will start being effective, but for maximum efficiency, you should empower each symbol for 9 days in a row. Thus, it is recommended that your first Kanji empowerment series, you should empower the symbols: Power, Hand and Spirit Energy, each for 15 minute. Then, you should empower the symbols for

Health, Happiness and Peace, which are always useful in most daily situations. You can empower as many new kanji you wish per day. If you wish to empower 6 kanji per day, it will take 1 hour and a half, for the entire nine days.

Hint: when meditating on Power/Riyoku, don't dwell on a feeling of superiority, but rather on the power in the universe. When meditating on Hand/Te, think of all that is to manipulate things, objects and energies. Always try to grasp the higher meaning of a concept, and a wider range of application. In this case, a hand can be a physical hand, and the philosophical hand of destiny, or even the hand of the Buddha (or God), if you allow yourself to be of a spiritual nature. The same with Spirit Energy/Se-i, you should try to let your Higher Self reveal to you what it means, while you are contemplating the possibilities of the higher nature of the concept. Empowerment is done thru meditation and contemplation, and not thru intellectualization.

In meditation, it is normal that your mind will wander and be distracted. This is a normal experience that all meditators go thru sometimes even for a few years. Don't worry about how much your mind collaborates to the experience. When you notice you are not focusing anymore on your Kanji empowerment, simply come back to it and try not to go about anymore. Yet, you will probably lose focus again, and simply come back again to the meditation.

Rules of the Art

The majutsushi must not only know the general rules, but also the art of Kuji-Kiri. While at first we must strive to follow the training rules as close as possible, when the user becomes an adept at the art, he must follow his intuition. Yet, too often intuition is invoked as a pretext to ridiculously alter the traditional ways into an experimental delusion of the inexperienced user. You are strongly encouraged to follow the guidelines until you grasp the feeling of Kuji-Kiri; until you can feel the system of Kuji-Kiri in your mind and in your body.

Once the rules are well anchored, it is time to un-anchor them. When you have learned and practiced Kuji-Kiri a lot, it will be time to release yourself from the rules, and allow yourself to express the spontaneous impulse from the soul. Yet, do not think you have attained this level of mastery within the first year.

General rules

Summarized: The mage will define and empower a desired effect, and use a physical anchor to link the spell to the target of the spell. The **symbols and signs** compose the spell. The **target** is the person, object or area to be affected. The **anchor** is a material item that is used to bind together the spell and the target.

Symbols: The most efficient way to cast a spell is to use a single symbol drawn over an obvious target. The symbols must represent the expected effect. The more global the effect, the easier it will be to cast, and the more efficient will be the spell. The general symbol of "health" will provide the desired effect. In this case, it is not required to indicate what to heal, like in drawing the symbols "health kidneys", since the grid and symbol can be drawn directly over the kidneys. It is encouraged not to use a symbol to designate a target, unless the target is unavailable.

Language: Learning Japanese as a language is not a necessity, but it will help you cast more complex spells. The non-Japanese speaker will be limited to single symbol grids, sometimes accompanied by very few support symbols. Yet, even the experienced majutsushi will usually prefer these simple spells, for they are usually the most efficient. Drawing too many symbols dilutes the effect of each one of them, spreading the willpower of the caster over a wider spell. Multiple symbols should be used when accuracy of the effect cannot be achieved with a single symbol, or when the target must be described in the spell, because of lack of availability.

Targets: If the target is available to the sight or touch, then the symbol simply has to be drawn over it. If the target is not available, you can draw the grid and symbol over a photo of the concerned target, or over an official paper representing the target.

When the target is not present, the way to affect it is to use a link to its energy signature. Any item belonging to the target is tainted with the energy signature of the target. A piece of clothing often worn by someone will suffice in linking a spell to a target. The more the target person was in contact with an object, the stronger the link will be. Emotions are the raw matter that builds those links. Thus, an item that was subject to a strong emotion will be more useful. The stronger the link to the energy signature of the target, the less energy of the spell is lost during the casting. You should have respect for the target if it is inappropriate to touch the area to affect (ie: when healing breast cancer). In such a case, you can figure out a way to affect the entire body, or use an anchor to tie the spell to the target.

Anchors: For a spell to last longer, it is useful to physically anchor it. You can physically anchor the spell by drawing the grid and symbol(s) with ink, either on a sheet of paper that the target will carry, or directly on an object that serves as a target link. Drawing only in the energy plane will have a temporary effect. A parchment can be easily attached to a target building, or in the vicinity of an area to affect. Anchors can also play a role in the casting of the spell. While using an anchor, might as well use material properties that will also support the effect of the spell. You cast the spell on a specific type of stone that corresponds to the desired effect, or use certain fabrics. You can perfume the anchor with scents that are recommended by aromatherapy. You can attach to the anchor other items that correspond to the target's energy signature. The possibilities are endless.

When fabricating a complex anchor, casting a spell on it will transform it into a talisman. You can find many of these corresponding components in other books about Mikkyo, or magic. The most important thing is that all the components of an anchor must be bonded together.

You can wrap a small parchment, put it in a small container, and tie it to someone or a building. If you use a holding device, like a string or chain, it should also be present at the moment of casting, so that it too will magically link the anchor to the target.

When using an anchor, the spells are unaffected by distance. In the Retsu level of Kuji-In, we learn that distance seems to exist in the phenomenal world, but it does not exist in the realms of consciousness. A good anchor will work around the globe, whether you know where the target is or not. However, the spell has its most powerful effect when it is casted, it will remain efficient and powerful for a while, but its effect will eventually start to diminish over time. For a spell to work over long periods of time, it is recommended to re-cast the spell periodically, or you can have the bearer repeat the words from time to time, while holding the talisman.

Will somewhat work: Drawing a grid and symbol in the midst of anywhere, using only visualization to cast the spell, while the target is not present, held only in the mind of the caster.

But the best would be: Using empowered items, drawing with ink of the recommended color on a parchment that will be held in contact with the target, and perfumed with the recommended aroma.

Influences: All that the caster does when he casts a spell, is to influence reality and illusion. The more powerful and experienced is the caster, the stronger the spell will alter the natural course of events, even beyond the natural laws. It takes much experience to influence the laws of nature, and it is always linked to a karmic price to pay. It is preferable to be compassionate in your work.

Elements: Everything in creation is made with the combinations of basic original elements. While elements are not always required in every spell, including them will greatly augment the spell's efficiency. The elemental influence should not be the main actor in the spell, unless it is based directly on a property inherent to the element. There are five elements from which creation came, and that compose all things. These elements are: earth, water, air, fire and void/spirit. It takes much time to charge in your consciousness and your soul, the energies of the five elements, but this empowerment makes everything so much more powerful. Even if an element is not included in a spell, each spell casted by a mage who has empowered the five elements will be greatly amplified. The process to empower the five elements requires the use of a mala. This process is provided at the end of this book.

Mala: A majutsushi usually has a charged mala, which is a Buddhist prayer necklace of exactly 108 beads. Sometimes there are other beads that serve as a counter locator, or a symbolic decoration, but the necklace loop must count 108 beads. (109 beads on a Hindu mala)

The soul (and mala) of the mage will eventually have to be charged with the nine Sanskrit mantras of Kuji-In. To charge a mala, the majutsushi chants each of the nine Sanskrit mantras of Kuji-In a total of 11664 times while counting with his mala. For twelve days in a row, without passing a single day, the majutsushi takes his mala, and chants the mantra using the beads to count, until he has chanted nine malas of a single mantra. A mala has 108 beads, chanted nine times per day (972 mantras) over a period of 12 days (11664 mantras). When the majutsushi has charged the first Kuji-In mantra (RIN), he then charges the second (KYO), and so on... After 108 days, the mala is charged, and so is the majutsushi.

If the majutsushi loses or permanently breaks his mala, he does not lose the charge he built in himself, this will never leave him. But he does lose the physical tool. A charged mala serves as a physical link to the matrix, greatly empowering the effect while cutting the grid. It is recommended that in such a case, a new mala be re-charged. Once your soul is charged, you do not need to go thru the entire process again, only to charge your new mala. To charge a new mala, you have to do 9 malas in a row of the mantra to be charged in the mala, and your soul will rebuild the influence it has on the new mala. You can also do 1 mala per day for 9 days.

Other mantras can be charged on the same mala. There are a few Buddhist mantras that will help the majutsushi in his practice. However, each new mantra charged on the mala used to do Kuji-Kiri, will prevent the casting of spells that are oriented in other directions. Charging the mantra of compassion will prevent the casting of harmful spells, but will positively influence the casting of every compassionate type spell. The mantra of compassion is: **Om Mani Padme Hum** .

A mala can only be used by the caster it belongs to. The caster must have charged his mala by himself, or in rare cases, when the mala is offered by an enlightened being that is "One" in consciousness with the majutsushi. In any case, the majutsushi must still have charged the nine mantras of Kuji-In in his own consciousness. The devoted majutsushi will also have to charge the five elements. This five element process can be found at the end of this book.

Preparation: Before any casting of a spell, the majutsushi must charge himself with the specific energies that will be required to cast the spell. This is done by:

- Meditating prior to the casting of the spell. Meditation is also recommended after the casting, for the sake of the caster.

- Chanting multiple malas of the Kuji-In mantra associated with the spell to cast, if it is known. We will often use the Kuji-In Sanskrit mantras. The elemental mantras can also be used, even if no element is present in the casting itself, it builds up raw matter in higher planes.

Casting: The caster must be relaxed before and after the casting. At the moment of casting, the majutsushi must empower himself spontaneously and become powerful in his behavior. All his actions must be filled with determination. His movements must not be stressed, angry or abrupt, but they must show self-control and strength. At the moment of casting, the majutsushi breathes in gracefully and powerfully, but not necessarily quickly. He braces his arms and torso, and the casting begins.

The grid must be drawn with confidence. It must not be drawn too swiftly, like if it was done with sword slashes, but rather done like if it was penetrating the fabric of the universe. Be as precise as possible, but do not worry about the exact graphic outcome. You must not permit your mind to have doubts about the spreads of the lines or the accuracy of the symbol. If you draw the grid and the symbol, it will work. Precision is something you must worry about when you practice, but during the actual casting, it must not even cross your mind.

While the grid is drawn, the caster has to be mentally and emotionally absorbed in the connection with the matrix of the universe. While the symbol is drawn, the caster has to be mentally and emotionally absorbed in the desired effect on the target.

When you are done drawing your symbol in the middle of the grid, place your entire palm in the grid and repeat the word(s) represented by the symbol(s) many times. The popular belief is that the majutsushi draws a grid and a symbol in midair, then utters a single word, but in actuality, it is recommended to keep your palm in the middle of the grid, and recite the spell at least of few times, while remaining totally absorbed in the desired effect. The casting is instantaneous only when using ink and paper. If you can permit yourself to be focused for at least one minute, it will have a much more powerful effect. In any case, re-cast the spell as often as possible, to nourish its effect, efficiency and duration. Use your mind to diffuse the effect of the new thought-form in the area to affect.

A very experienced majutsushi can cast a spell without preparation, without anchor to the target, in a swift manner, without even uttering the spell vocally. This requires practice and experience. You should first start by drawing the grid slowly, followed by the symbol, in a paused manner. If you draw multiple symbols, utter the complete word/spell once at the end of the drawing process. Don't hesitate to pull willpower into your intention, but do not allow your heart and guts to become enraged or negative. Power can remain pure in intention and will.

Spell casting examples will be provided later in the book, so that you can get a better idea of how the entire process goes. It will be useful to reread this entire document a few times.

Shapes and signs

Other shapes and symbols can be used as a form of support for the main influence of a process. In Kuji-Kiri, while the most important aspect of a process consists in drawing the main symbol over the grid, it is common to see other symbols under the grid, or on the other side of a talisman. We will often see different shapes and sings, accompanied by other kanji.

Whenever possible, try to draw shapes and signs in a clockwise fashion. Draw a single line from top to bottom, or from left to right. Draw other shapes from their upper left (or central) point, and to the right and bottom. An upright triangle would be drawn from the upper central tip, to the bottom right, to the bottom left, and back to the upper central tip. While a downward triangle would be drawn from the upper left tip, to the upper right, to the central bottom, and back to the upper left tip. When placed flat on the floor or in a horizontally fixed anchor, you should use the magnetic north to define the top orientation of the entire design.

In the intensity of the moment, do not expect to draw perfectly straight lines. Do your best to be as symmetric and coherent as possible, but also accept the slight variations, that will nonetheless add style to the art. Closed shapes (circle, triangle, square...) should not have any opening or be missing any part of the shape. Closed shapes must be entirely closed when drawn. For all these reasons, you will have to practice your drawing skills with your hand, but also with your pen/brush on paper. Take some time to practice making lots of circles, and lots of triangles, and lots of squares, so that you get better and better. Then, at the moment of an actual ritual or spell-casting, you will be better than if you had not practiced at all.

Each shape must be empowered the same way you did with the empowerment of symbols, drawing them in front of you, dragging them in your mind/nervous system, your abdomen, and your entire body, and meditating. Repeat the shape empowerments for 9 days for maximum efficiency.

Vertical line: A line can be drawn vertically to separate two effects, or define a limit of influence. Its use is not common.

Horizontal line: A line can be drawn horizontally to indicate a physical and spiritual combination of forces, when a symbol is drawn over and under it. A horizontal line at the bottom of a formula or spell can indicate that it stands on natural laws or physical principles, or to bring stability to a situation.

Triangle: A triangle can be drawn to promote the expansion of a certain conceptual energy. A kanji drawn inside the triangle will be the force in expansion, while 3 small kanji drawn outside its faces will represent the result of the expansion. A triangle pointing down will bring spiritual energies to lower, more tangible planes, while a triangle pointing upwards will indicate a rising force, an uplifting, or a spiritualizing experience.

A good rising triangle example is to draw the kanji of fire inside the upright triangle, then the kanji of purity below it, the kanji of harmony on the left, and kanji of happiness on the right. Put all this in a circle, and you have a talisman to purify energies, emotions and thoughts, that will bring a sense of harmony in your mind and happiness in your heart.

Square: Mostly used in physical or tangible matters, the square represents the spiritual base for physical form. The square is the

archetypal block that composes structures. It is used to address the physical plane. It is often used as the most outward shape. In Buddhist and Hindu mandalas, it is common to see a circle base in the center of a general design, representing spiritual events or concepts, encased in a square exterior shape that represents the world, the structure, or the physical manifestation. The square is most often a philosophical container of some sort, like the physical body, an energy reserve, a house, or other.

Cross: The balanced cross is similar to the square concept, for it is still a shape based on the number 4. It is used to represent the spiritual and physical plane interacting. It is also used to represent the structure, where the square is used to represent the container.

Swastika: This shape is the cross in movement, representing the world in motion. Its right angles mean that the structural energies are in motion. It is used to bring luck, blessing, and ensure that every aspect of a situation is

working well. It is popular in Hinduism and Buddhism. It is often seen in the hand of a holy figure. Although it was made popular with the Nazi movement, it should not distract you from the beauty and integrity of this most ancient holy shape. The swastika has been used since the origins of spiritual traditions for good luck, prosperity and victory. The Buddhist swastika, aimed at elevating the human self to the spiritual reality, is drawn like it is shown here. But the Hindu swastika was used to bring spiritual energies in the tangible experience, and the direction of the branches are in the other direction (like the Nazi symbol was).

Pentagon: The more complex the shapes become, the more difficulty it adds to the empowerment and the spell-casting. Its understanding is essential before you can start using it in ritual magic or spell-casting. While the square, 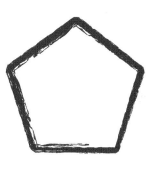 based on the number 4, is the final step of any type of manifestation in the world, the pentagon, based on the number 5, represents the resultant of a manifested experience. You should use the pentagon if you wish to influence the outcome of a physical action, or of a structural process. Place a Kanji inside the shape representing the result you wish to obtain as the outcome of an action or event. If you insist in putting kanji or symbols outside the shape, they should describe the way you wish the events to happen. If you wish to add even more precisions, know that the upper right side is about the spiritualized emotional force, the upper left side is the intellectual understanding, the lower right side is the humanized artistic or sensuous aspect, the lower left side is the mechanical understanding of the process, and the bottom side is about the physical act, container or event itself. When you first empower the pentagon, you should simply empower the general shape and try to grasp its concept, without paying attention to the function of each side. At a later time, when you are more experienced, you should re-empower the pentagon when you can remember the five outer aspects mentioned.

You should avoid using too complex of structures in your first attempts at Majutsu ritual or spell-casting. Nonetheless, before you can efficiently empower further shapes, like the pentagon or the pentagram, the first shapes to be empowered should be the circle, triangle, square and cross.

Pentagram: Like the pentagon, the pentagram, also based on the number 5, is complex and difficult to grasp at first. While the pentagon is a closed shape encompassing its entire inner area, the pentagram crosses each line over two  other lines, representing the interaction of forces. Once a shape is manifested or set in place (square, cross, 4), it can be set in motion with the pentagram, which is the interactive 5 sided shape. While the pentagon is used to address and direct the natural motion of things, the pentagram is used to create an influence, to willingly set a force in motion, or to powerfully resist another force. The pentagram is used to control an element, to produce events, to apply your will over something, to provoke a motion in a situation that was previously inactive. The pentagram is probably the most difficult shape to understand and empower completely. When you are ready to empower the pentagram, you should first empower it only using the general concept of setting forces in motion. It will be sufficient to use it in your art by placing a kanji in its center. However, if you wish to go a second step, know that the signification of the outer spaces inbetween each tip are similar to the sides of the pentagon. To go one more step further, the inner spaces in each tip works as follows. The upper tip will represent the higher nature, the Self, the most spiritual aspect. The upper left tip will represent the raw or basic force in motion. The upper right tip will represent the method or strategy of the motion. The lower left tip will represent the way the raw force will influence the physical event. The lower right tip will represent the feeling or emotional charge behind the motion. In any case, the pentagram will be most effective if you empower it three times; once with the general shape, a second time with the concepts of the outer tips (similar to pentagon), and a third time with the concepts of the inner tips.

Generally, we place a pentagram inside a circle for a general influence in every aspect. The circled pentagram is used in many talismans, and is very easy to use as a medallion. However, you can place the pentagram in a square, with no tips touching the square, to represent a force set in motion in the most tangible way. The pentagram can be placed inside a pentagon, tips touching the outer shape or not, to have a maximum precision in the effect of the talisman. However, you should be warned that the more complex your talisman becomes, the less effective it is if you can't grasp all the aspects of a talisman in a single thought form. For this reason, you should avoid creating pizza-like talismans such as a triangle in the center of pentagram which is also in the center of a square, with a sea of kanji, symbols, crosses and swastikas floating around, in every free corner of a most impressive design. To better illustrate what we mean, please try to analyze and understand the entire concept shown below, which is supposed to bring wealth thru easy work, if it can actually be drawn by a majutsushi capable of keeping everything in mind during the drawing and spell-casting of the talisman.

Below is a standard application of pentagram talisman. I'll let you discover the inner workings when you have gained much more experience in Majutsu, but I'll tell you it has to do with rectifying ones karmic weight, to release the manifestation of suffering in one's life.

Even if you did not yet empower each aspect of this talisman, the reproduction of it along with a simple empowerment will still have its positive effect. This talisman could be drawn on the other side of a parchment baring a Kuji-Kiri grid with the symbol of happiness.

6 pointed star: Combining the effect of two triangles joining, we can deduct that it has to do with the joining of two expansive complementary forces. The upright triangle going up to the spiritual realm, and the downward triangle going towards the physical aspect, they join at a point of convergence, and bind together harmoniously. This shape always represents the harmony of polarities, the collaboration of all levels of an experience, and the unity of consciousness in every aspect of a situation. It can be used to help in the joining of a man and a woman, but you should abstain from casting spells that go against someone's free will. It can be used in strengthening the bonds of a family. It is useful in spiritual matters where we wish to unite our human nature to the Higher Self, or even to bring the presence of the Self in the tangible experience of life. The two triangles will always represent polarities. The downward triangle comes from the heavens and thus represents the masculine, the positive aspect, daytime, Yang, incarnation… while the upright triangle comes from the earth and represents the feminine, the negative polarity, nighttime, Yin, sublimation…

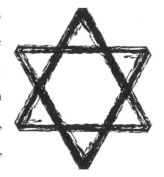

The inner center area is the place of the Self, of the goal of the influence, or the main acting character in the talisman. The 6 inner areas of each point represent forces in action. The 6 outer spaces in-between each tip represent the way the events will take place, or the energies accompanying the manifestation.

The 6 inner areas in the points, combined with the 6 outer areas in-between the tips, are 12 areas that each have their function. These spaces can be used to display the 12 signs of the zodiac, or a series of symbols that will influence the happening of an event. Symbols can also be placed at the tip of each point if there is room, to represent the resulting outcome of the inner forces at work in the inner tips. Remember that too much complexity might take you away from your goal. The simpler the talisman, the better it is.

The 6-pointed star is always existential in its use. It is rarely used in oriental magic. Because of its binding properties, it did not become popular amongst the Buddhist mages that promoted non-attachment. Where the Hindus want to unite the body with the Spirit, the Buddhists wish to detach from all material things, including their own body, eventually. Nonetheless, it is useful to use this shape in family matters, amongst groups, in a community, or in a relationship.

Empowering Kuji-In kanji

Before you empower more symbols, you should empower the nine basic Kuji-In Kanji, simply to make them more present in your Kuji-Kiri practice, and make the drawing of the grid more efficient.

RIN (Face, Meet)   KYO (Strategy)   TOH (Fight)
Rin (リン)   Hiyou (ヒョウ)   TOu(トウ)

SHA (Person)
Shia (シャ)

KAI (All)
Kai (カイ)

JIN (Position)
Jin (ジン)

者 皆 陣

RETSU (Split, line)
Retsu (レツ)

ZAI (Exist)
Zai (ザイ)

ZEN (In front)
Zen (ゼン)

列 在 前

Sample applications

The popular application of Kuji-Kiri nowadays is to accompany a conventional treatment for health benefits, or to protect a house. Nonetheless, we will cover a few sample applications so that you get to understand the general rules. Yet it does not suffice to know the rules, you also have to practice for a great while, so to synchronize your visualization, gestures, and willpower.

Simple ritual

Here is an example of how a user would set a protection circle for his home. The symbol of protection will be the main symbol drawn on the grid, and the symbol of harmony will accompany the talisman, drawn over a simple rice paper sheet. We consider here that the symbols of protection and harmony are already empowered by the user, thru previous meditation. The brush, ink and sheet have been previously empowered for a short moment, right before the ritual itself.

- User has prepared a traditional Japanese brush, sheet of rice paper, and black ink. He is in his house. He can light a white candle and some soft incense.
- User meditates for five minutes on the symbols of protection and harmony, and their radiance pervading his

house, using as a mantra the recitation of the words in Japanese (Ei... wa...). Very experienced majutsushi do not have to meditate prior to a Kuji-Kiri process, especially if they are permanently in a meditative state.

- User slowly comes out of the meditative state, not to give a shock to his nervous system, but does not lose the focus on the concept he is empowering.

- User snaps into an empowered state of mind with will power, taking a deep breath, erecting his spine for a moment, opening his eyes wide.

- Immediately takes the brush and draws the Kuji-Kiri grid on the upper part of the rice paper sheet, while reciting the nine syllables (Visualization of the Kuji-In kanji is not essential, and would be difficult considering the speed of the drawing). It has to be done in a decisive, yet non violent way.

- User takes more ink, and draws the symbol of protection over the center of the grid. A symbol does not have to touch all lines, but only be within it. At the last stroke(s) of this symbol, he utters or shouts the Japanese word (Ei) with great will power in his voice and mind.

- He then draws the symbol of harmony under the grid, staying focused but pushing less will and intention. On the last stroke, he utters or shouts the Japanese word (wa). The voice must imitate the attitude of the word, thus there can't be anger in shouting "Wa!!!". In this case, a soft but decided uttering is recommended.

The talisman sheet is now empowered and is ready to affix to a part of the foundation of the house. If the house would be under a specific threat, then it would be recommended to make as much of those talismans, in a small format, to place above each door and window.

Complex ritual

For this sample ritual, the majutsushi will be performing an abundance blessing for someone else, in a way to create a talisman that the specific receiver will be able to wear on him/herself.

The mage will have a brush and black ink. He will prepare a rice paper sheet cut to the size of 2"x2". He will fold the sheet in four, so that once unfolded, the sheet will still have the markings of the folding, making visible four squares of 1"x1". The relation to the number 4 should be clear at this point. The goal of this process is to bring manifesting energies to the physical plane.

He will also have a bottle of essential oil of orange, or of another plant that represents abundance. A small fabric pouch will be used to put the folded talisman. Four orange or white candles will be lit in each direction, around the mage and the spell-casting area. For this ritual, the mage will need a small photo of the target person who will be carrying the talisman in the pouch. The photo will be placed on the altar, table, or casting area. The talisman paper will be put over the photo. The target on the photo will also be empowered while the mage draws the symbols on the paper over it.

The user will do about the same as in the prior simple ritual, with the symbols of abundance, wealth and happiness. The user will snap out of the meditative state to draw the grid on the inner side of the 2"x2" paper. He will then cast the symbol of wealth over the grid, in a decisive and artistic manner, shouting "FU" on his last brush stroke. He will proceed to blow on the ink to make it dry faster. While blowing for 1 minute, might as well transmit more energy to the talisman by visualizing the vibration of wealth investing the talisman thru the blown wind. Once the ink looks dry enough, the mage will fold the talisman one time, the left side folding on the right side. He will put a drop of orange essential oil, previously empowered. He will then fold the upper part on the lower part of the talisman, bringing it to the final 1"x1" size. On the front side, he will draw the kanji of abundance, blow on it to make it dry, while empowering more with abundance. Then he will turn the talisman to expose the back side, onto which he will cast the symbol of happiness. He will blow again to help the ink dry faster.

The photo of the target and the talisman will be put together in the small fabric pouch, or other suitable container. The presence of the photo is to keep empowering the target even when the talisman is not worn by, or carried close to the target.

If the majutsushi wishes, he can take a bit of time to explain what he did to the receiver. It is wise to plant the seeds of consciousness in the mind of those who are ready to understand them. However, be humble and diligent with elder people, or those who could be offended by knowing the details of the art.

Symbol appendix

RIN related

The first set of symbols relate mostly to the base chakra type of experience. These symbols would be visualized as red, either glowing, fiery or striking red lightning, depending on the type of effect you wish for. The base chakra manages all the areas that relate to being alive, powerful, and present in the body. It relates to issues of physical security, to genetic behaviors, and much more. All that is covered in the RIN Kuji-In chapters relate to the base chakra.

Trust	Faith	Life
Shin (シン)	Ko-u (コウ)	Mei (メイ)

KYO related

The second set of symbols relate mostly to the navel chakra. These symbols can be visualized in orange, for internal purposes, and with white flows of light, for interaction with the world. Note that if you wish to bring someone's internal energy to rise up, you should use the orange visualization related to internal purposes. The fact that your target is someone else does not mean it is an "interaction" type of application. The visualization does not depend on how the target/receiver relates to you, but how it relates to the desired effect. The second series of symbols relate to experiences similar to the KYO Kuji-In.

Control	Master	Justice
Katsu (カツ)	Shiyu (シユ)	Gi (ギ)

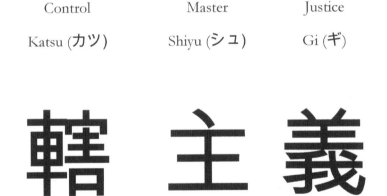

TOH related

The TOH type symbols should be visualized in white light. Its source is the inner abdomen, the dan-tian. It can be visualized in the abdomen, or around the body, or target. It is used to conquer oneself, to fight our inner demons. Only when we are victorious within, can we become victorious without.

Victory	Harmony	Protection
Shiyou (ショウ)	Wa (ワ)	Ei (エイ)

勝　和　衛

SHA related

The SHA related symbols should be visualized yellow for intellectual affairs, and golden for spiritual or healing matters. It has a relation with the solar plexus.

Healthy	Illuminate	Determination
Ken (ケン)	Shiyou (ショウ)	Ketsu (ケツ)

健 照 決

Note: The victory sign in the Kyo series is said the same way as Shine/illuminate, of the Sha series. It is like a homonym. Same goes for many others, like the word "Shin" for truth, and heart.

KAI related

The KAI related symbols should be visualized as bright emerald green. Its relation is to the heart. It is used to discover Love within. Only then can it be expressed outside.

Love	Affection	Heart
Ai (アイ)	Ji (ジ)	Shin (シン)

Compassion

Dou (ドウ) Jiyou (ジョウ)

JIN related

The JIN related symbols should be visualized as bright electric blue. Its relation is to the throat chakra. They relate mostly in understanding oneself, understanding the world, knowledge, expression…

Understand	Knowledge	Wisdom
Chi (チ)	Kaku (カク)	Ei (エイ)

知　覚　叡

RETSU related

The RETSU related symbols should be visualized as dark green, or luminous jade green. Its relation is to the jade gate, behind the skull. The goal of these symbols makes little sense to the inexperienced spiritualist. They mostly relate to perception, dimension, space and time.

Perception	Space	Time
Nin (ニン)	Ku-u (クウ)	Ki (キ)

ZAI related

The ZAI related symbols should be visualized as light radiating dark indigo, similar to a white/mauve luminous stroke, with the haze of a black light. These symbols relate to the third eye, to the concepts of spirituality and creation.

Create	Element	Origin / source
Sou (ソウ)	so(ソ)	Gen (ゲン)

創　素　元

A base/original element is also Genso (ゲンソ) 元素

An elemental being is Gensoshia(ゲンソシャ) 元素者

ZEN related

The ZEN related symbols should be visualized as light radiating, mostly white and golden. It has a relation with the crown chakra.

Buddha

Butsu (ブツ)

Truth

Shin (シン)

Heaven

Ten (テン)

佛 真 天

Meditation

Mei (メイ)

Angel / Celestial

Tenshi (テンシ)

瞑 天使

The Elements

Earth	Water	Wind
Chi (チ)	Sui (スイ)	Fu (フウ)

地 水 風

Fire	Void
Ka (カ)	Ku-u (クウ)

火 空

Other Useful Kanji

Word	Romanji	Katakana	Kanji
Abundance	Ho-u	ホウ	豊
Acceptance	Yo-u	ヨウ	容
Buddha	Butsu	ブツ	佛
Forgive	Shia	シャ	赦
Physical	Tai	タイ	体
Recognition	Nin	ニン	認
Relationship	Chiyu-u	チュウ	仲

Responsible/answer to	Seki	セキ	責
Responsibility / duty	Nin	ニン	任
Sincerity	Sei	セイ	誠
Spirit / soul	Rei	レイ	霊
Wealth	Fu	フ	富

For more kanji, you should search the web, or purchase a kanji dictionary. Empowering all the kanji found in this book, in the suggested order, will give you the most direct experience of what it is to become a majutsushi.

Kuji-In

For those who are not interested yet in developing the full potential of Kuji-In, here is the most basic introduction. Kuji-In is an art that transforms the practitioner into a supernatural being. Yet, for the curious, this short introduction will suffice for basic empowerment of the Kuji-Kiri grid.

Only the Japanese pronunciation of the mantras is provided. The original Sanskrit version is to be used by the most devoted users of Kuji-In.

Put yourself in a relaxed or meditative state, then put your hands in the suggested mudra form, and repeat the mantra for long periods, while contemplating the short philosophical principles of each step of Kuji-In.

Each Ji-In (syllable seal) must be practiced for a minimum of a few hours so that your soul may become charged with the spiritual energies they invoke. Cutting the grid is next to useless before this process is done. It is only when Kuji-In is activated in you that the grid really interfaces with the fabric of the universe while you draw it.

1- RIN

Extend your two middle fingers and interlace all other fingers.

Chakra: Base

Mantra jp: On baï shi ra man ta ya sowaka

The RIN set is used to strengthen your mind and body. This Kuji-In set must be performed before any other Kuji-In sets can truly be effective. The RIN Kuji acts as a sort of hook-up to the Ultimate Source of all Power. By connecting you with this Divine energy, the RIN Kuji strengthens your mind and body, especially in collaboration with the other practices of the Kuji-In. A stronger connection to the Divine energy source will make you stronger at every level. Please be aware that this set may elevate your body temperature.

2- KYO

Extend your index fingers and bend your middle fingers over your index fingers so that the tip of your thumbs are touching. Interlace all your other fingers.

Chakra: Hara/Navel

Mantra jp:　　On isha na ya in ta ra ya sowaka

KYO activates the flow of energy within your body and outside of you, in your environment. This Kuji will help you learn to direct energy throughout your body, and eventually outside your body, so you can manifest your desires in the objective world. Although willpower directs energy, you must not push too hard with your willpower. Willpower that is used to direct energy should be rather like "wanting something a lot" but not like "getting a stranglehold on something, or pushing with a crippling force". Even when you apply your willpower to attain something you desire, you must always be at peace and relaxed.

3- TOH

Point your thumbs and the last two fingers of both hands while keeping your index and middle fingers interlaced inside your hands.

Chakra: Dan-tian, between the Hara and the Solar Plexus
Mantra jp: On je te ra shi ita ra ji ba ra ta no-o sowaka

By practicing TOH, you will develop your relationship with your immediate environment, and eventually with the entire universe. As you practice, begin by filling yourself with energy and then surround yourself with this energy. (This is accomplished by visualizing that it is so). This is the Kuji of harmony. It teaches you to accept the outside events of life while remaining at peace inside. Always breathe deeply inside your abdomen, naturally, without strain.

4- SHA

Extend your thumbs, index fingers and both little fingers. Interlace your middle and fourth finger inside your hands.

Chakra: Solar Plexus
Mantra jp: On ha ya baï shi ra man ta ya sowaka

With this Kuji, the healing ability of your body is increased. As you practice this set, your body will become more efficient in its daily rebuilding, healing and reconstruction. This increased healing efficiency is the result of the higher levels of energy passing through your energy channels (Meridians) and your solar plexus. This healing vibration will eventually radiate around you, causing other people to heal as you spend time with them.

5- KAI

Interlace all of your fingers, with the tip of each finger pressing into the root of the facing finger.

Chakra: Heart

Mantra jp: On no-o ma ku san man da ba sa ra dan kan

This Kuji will raise your awareness and help you to develop your intuition. The mudra is called "The outer bonds". The outer bonds are the energy currents that precede every event, if only for an instant. They are the specific influence from the outside world that produces every one of your experiences.

Intuition is a powerful ally; it is the way you perceive what your senses register from your contact with the environment, and from the people surrounding you. This set will increase your intuition and will help you to learn to love yourself and others.

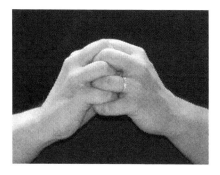 

Interlace all your fingers, with your fingertips inside, each of them touching the equivalent tip of the other hand's finger, if possible.

Chakra: Throat

Mantra jp: On aga na ya in ma ya sowaka

The "inner bonds" are the energy currents inside you that connect you with your True Self. We have the ability to know what others are thinking. By reaching deep inside you, into the place with no words, you may get in contact with this same place in others. When you make this connection you may hear the other person's thoughts without words, or you may learn to communicate by thought concepts; this is commonly called telepathy.

7- RETSU

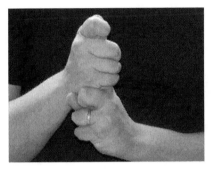

Point your left index finger up. Wrap the fingers of your right hand around your left index finger. Place the tips of your right thumb and index finger in contact with the tip of your left index finger. The fingers of your left hand are gathered into a fist.

Chakra: Jade Gate, at the back of the head
Mantra jp: On hi ro ta ki sha no ga ji ba tai sowaka

After practicing the Kuji-In exercises for some time, they will alter your perception of gross matter so you will be able to perceive the different flows of energy composing our space-time multi-dimensional universe. Per the theory of relativity, as mass accelerates, time slows, thus if your energy is flowing, and you apply your willpower, your mass accelerates, time slows for you and you can simply change (or direct) the flow/ or motion of your body through space.

8- ZAI

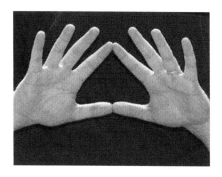

Touch the tips of your thumbs and index fingers to form a triangle, while your other fingers are spread out.

Chakra: Third Eye
Mantra jp: On Chi ri Chi i ba ro ta ya sowaka

By practicing with this set, you will establish a relationship with the Universal components of creation: the elements. These elements are not only physical, they are also spiritual. This Kuji practice is a basis for the power of manifestation. Visualize being in harmony with nature. Visualize the flow of Qi from nature to you, and from you to nature. After a while, notice your increasing awareness that nature is alive, and that you can communicate with it. Nature will interact with you within the limits of natural law. Eventually, as you improve your sensitivity to nature, you might develop the ability to call forth an elemental manifestation, when mastered.

9- ZEN

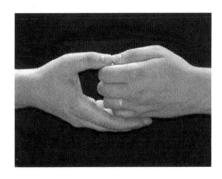

Rest your left knuckles on the fingers of your right hand, with your right palm open. Touch the tips of your two thumbs gently.

Chakra: Crown

Mantra jp: On a ra ba sha no-o sowaka

Illumination is the highest state of mind. Illumination is a kind of Completeness, accomplished by Meditation. By using this practice, you can eventually disappear from the common mind. You are still there, of course, but others in the common mind cannot register your presence, because your vibration is higher than what their minds can recognize or interpret as real. To practice, imagine simple emptiness, calm white light everywhere; Then visualize melding with the white light. It is believed that to the average person you might become invisible.

Many hours of practice are required to elevate your vibration level enough to manifest the side-effects, like suggestive invisibility.

The 5 Elements

In addition to empowering yourself with the kanji of each of the five elements, it is required to charge the energy of the elements in your soul. In this case, it will be done like the Buddhist mages do so, with the use of a mala. A mala is a wood bead necklace of exactly 108 beads. Some have a 109th bead that is not counted during this practice. The expression "chanting a mala" means that you will chant, or speak rapidly, a certain mantra for exactly 108 times, while using your mala to count. Use your thumb or major to count the beads. You should not use your index finger to shift the beads while reciting mantras.

The five elements are more than the tangible elements we think of when we speak of earth, fire, spirit, water and air. The spiritual five elements refer to their concept, rather than their physical manifestation. We will explain the concepts to contemplate while you charge the mantras of the five elements. The following concepts are what I like to refer to as the basic five elements, where we go to the core of their energy. For each of the five elements, you will do a 9 x 12 type charge, reciting 9 malas per day, or 35 minutes, each day for 12 days in a row. Using a mala goes a bit faster than counting 35 minutes, when you are used to the spelling of the mantras.

Each of the five elements mantras call forth the assistance of Divine concepts that most people refer to as gods. We do not require the belief that there are actual human people in the personal forms of Bhumidevi, Agni, Avalokiteshwara, Tara, Cittaamala... These are the representation of the highest forces acting in the universe, and these mantras use the Buddhist approach to invoking their intervention. There are no real elemental processes that do not invoke the help of the Divine forces. However, everyone may call upon the Divine names of their own system of belief. We will provide an explanation of each mantra, and offer variation possibilities, for the student to call the Divine forces using the names that correspond to their system of belief.

A student once asked me if it was acceptable to charge more than one mantra at a time. About charging more than one mantra at a time, you may, while following a simple rule. When charging mantras from series (like the elements) you have to be certain to start the mantra charges in order to finish charging each mantra before you finish the next one following it. Start the fire mantra charge after you start the earth mantra charge, so that you finish the fire charge after you finish the earth charge. This also means that if you charge the earth and fire elements in the same twelve days, you simply have to do the earth mantra first, and the fire mantra charge next. The same goes for charging the 9 Kuji-In mantras (not doing the Kuji-In mudra while you hold you mala).

Earth

Most people will think of earth as a symbol of stability, while the spiritual concept of earth is generation. Stability is linked mostly to the symbol of a rock, which is a part of the earth element. From the earth comes life, and it contains all the metals that manage electro-magnetic fields. Earth does encompass the concept of stability, but it goes so much further. The earth element is the most important element to keep elevated in your energy system. It is the base of creation, and it is also the base of mental health. Have you ever seen a "down-to-earth" person with mental illness? Most mentally ill people are not connected to the earth element.

While you charge the earth element, or simply recite the mantra, think of the life-giving aspect, the generation of plants, and the support of electro-magnetic fields. The earth element will stabilize and purify your Chi, your life energy. It will support protection circles around you, at the physical and spiritual levels.

The earth mantra: Om prithividhatu Bhumideviya

Om: Divine syllable

Prithivi: earth, the dirt

Dhatu: nature of, aspect of

Bhum: earth, the planet

Devi: divinity

Ya: grammatical association

The earth mantra invokes the energy of the earthly nature of the divine being that is our planet. All traditions may recite this mantra and respect their tradition. The English translation would be something like "earthly nature of the goddess Earth".

Once you have charged the earth mantra, you will be able to invoke protection energies each time you recite the mantra mentally or aloud. Your mental health will increase. Your paranoia will disappear. Your Chi / Life force will flow harmoniously in your body. The earth element is an essential before we can proceed to other trainings that involve interaction with the material world.

Fire

The fire element is NOT the concept of burning and destruction, although it can be used for such applications, mostly in purification processes. The fire element's true form is not destructive. Fire takes matter from a certain level of vibration, and it brings it to another higher level. Fire elevates the energies. It purifies the dense stagnant energies and transforms them in a higher nature, unclogging your energy circuitry. Fire also brings change and renewal.

In nature, we can observe how fire will transform solid compounds into liquid or gaseous forms. It alters the molecular structure and the chemical formulation of components. Fire generates energy, and makes every other process powerful.

While you use the fire mantra, contemplate the power-generating forces, and the elevating effect.

The fire mantra: Om Tejasdhatu Agnaya

Om: Divine syllable

Tejas: Power, energy, force associated to fire

Dhatu: nature of, aspect of

Agni: Fire, both the form and Divinity (Agnaya here)

Ya: grammatical association

Agni is not a Divinity limited to any tradition. It is more popular in the Hindu tradition, but it simply means fire, in the form of an intelligent natural force. Fire is the most powerful force in nature. This mantra means something like "Powerful nature of Fire". In sanskrit, sometimes we write the word Fire using "tejas" and sometimes using "agni".

Heaven

The heaven element is of the highest spiritual nature. It invokes the action of God in your life. It is the spiritual element. It is the tool of all spiritual activity. Charging this mantra elevates your consciousness. If you are not already born (fully existing) in the spiritual realm, this mantra will accelerate the process.

The Heaven mantra: Om Akashadhatu Avalokiteshwaraya

Om: Divine syllable

Akahsa: Heavens, spiritual realms

Dhatu: nature of, aspect of

Avalokiteshwara: Bodhisattva of compassion

Ya: grammatical association

Avalokiteshwara is the third personalized concept of the Holy trinity in Buddhism. Where the Christians name the "Father, Christ, Holy Spirit", the Hindu name the "Bramha, Vishnu,

Shiva". The Buddhist would see the trinity of their concepts in "Amitabha, Mahastamaprapta, Avalokiteshwara".

If you feel uncomfortable praying to Avalokiteshwara using the Buddhist mantra, you can recite the mantra using the name of the Christian Holy Spirit/Ghost said in Sanskrit like so:
Om Akashadhatu Baghavaatman

Or using the equivalent in the Hindu tradition:
Om Akashadhatu Shivaya

Water

In water, life is born. Water is the supporting substance in which all life dwells. Water fashions earth. Water is the element that represents the womb of the universe. All is within a form of water of a higher nature that encompasses, penetrates and pervades the entire universe. There is no matter that exists without this primeval water. It is the infinite light of creation, in a tangible form. It is the base constituent of Chi and life force.

The water process connects you with life, movement, and the universe. It is in this primeval water that we extend our consciousness. Charging the water mantra connects us to the flow of life. It purifies our body, heart and mind. It soothes our aches, it cares for us.

The water mantra: Om Apsadhatu Taraya

Om: Divine syllable

Apsa: water

Dhatu: nature of, aspect of

Tara: Divine mother

Ya: grammatical association

The name Tara(ya) can be changed to the Christian name of the Divine mother, Maria(ya), or the Hindu name Durga(ya).

Once you have charged the water mantra, the effects will become available naturally. Your level of energy (life) will increase. Your heart will be more stable, while your mind will become more flexible. Charging the water mantra give your healing ability a great boost. It supports all manifestations.

Air

It is thru air that information is shared, and movement takes place. Air supports all kinds of vibration while altering them the least. Air lets light thru. The air is where sounds travel. The air mantra opens your mind and other senses to information. It helps you perceive in every way. It also takes part in any kind of traveling and motion. The air mantra will also free your mind from limiting thoughts. It will broaden your perception of the universe and of yourself.

The Air mantra: Om Vayudhatu Cittaamalaya

Om: Divine syllable

Vayu: air / wind

Dhatu: nature of, aspect of

Cittaamala: Pure-minded

Ya: grammatical association

The mind is like a monkey, always jumping everywhere. We aim at mastering our mind so that our thoughts become focused. The Hindu monkey god Hanuman is not a person, but a representation of the mastered mind, or the mind taken under our own control, and dominated by our Spirit. The Hindu will use the name Hanumanta(ya), which is the son of the Monkey God, invoking a stable and pure mind.

Charging the five elements can take as little as 60 days, if you do 9 malas per day for 12 days, for the five elements in a row. Charging the five elements will awaken every aspect of your spirituality. It will give a biological wisdom to your body. It will open spiritual doors, release blockages, purify your energies.

The five elements are an important part of teaching your mind, heart and body, to interact with nature and go beyond its illusionary limitations. Nature was created with the spiritual concepts of the five elements. It is still operated by the elemental forces.

Charging the five elements will give you the basic tools required to advance much faster in any other training you do; physical, mental or spiritual. Once you have charged the five elements, it is recommended to do activation or support malas from time to time, to keep their energies active and intense in your body. Every now and then, do five malas in a row, one mala of each of the five elements.

The five elements must be fully charged before you can start using them. Until you learn how to use these energies, keep them for yourself. They will support every other spiritual action you take. Once you have learned the benefits of the elemental energies, you can use them to treat other people who lack these energies, by touch or transmigration. After a treatment, you must purify your own energies.

Hiragana Chart

	A	I	U	E	O
	あ	い	う	え	お
K	か	き	く	け	こ
S	さ	し	す	せ	そ
T	た	ち	つ	て	と
N	な	に	ぬ	ね	の
H	は	ひ	ふ	へ	ほ
M	ま	み	む	め	も
Y	や		ゆ		よ
R	ら	り	る	れ	ろ
W	わ	ゐ		ゑ	を
N					ん

Katakana Chart

	A	I	U	E	O
	ア	イ	ウ	エ	オ
K	カ	キ	ク	ケ	コ
S	サ	シ	ス	セ	ソ
T	タ	チ	ツ	テ	ト
N	ナ	ニ	ヌ	ネ	ノ
H	ハ	ヒ	フ	ヘ	ホ
M	マ	ミ	ム	メ	モ
Y	ヤ		ユ		ヨ
R	ラ	リ	ル	レ	ロ
W	ワ	ヰ		ヱ	ヲ
N					ン